ALEXANDER THE GREAT

MACEDONIAN KING AND CONQUEROR

Leaders of the Ancient World

ALEXANDER THE GREAT

MACEDONIAN KING AND CONQUEROR

Beatriz Santillian and
Bernard Randall

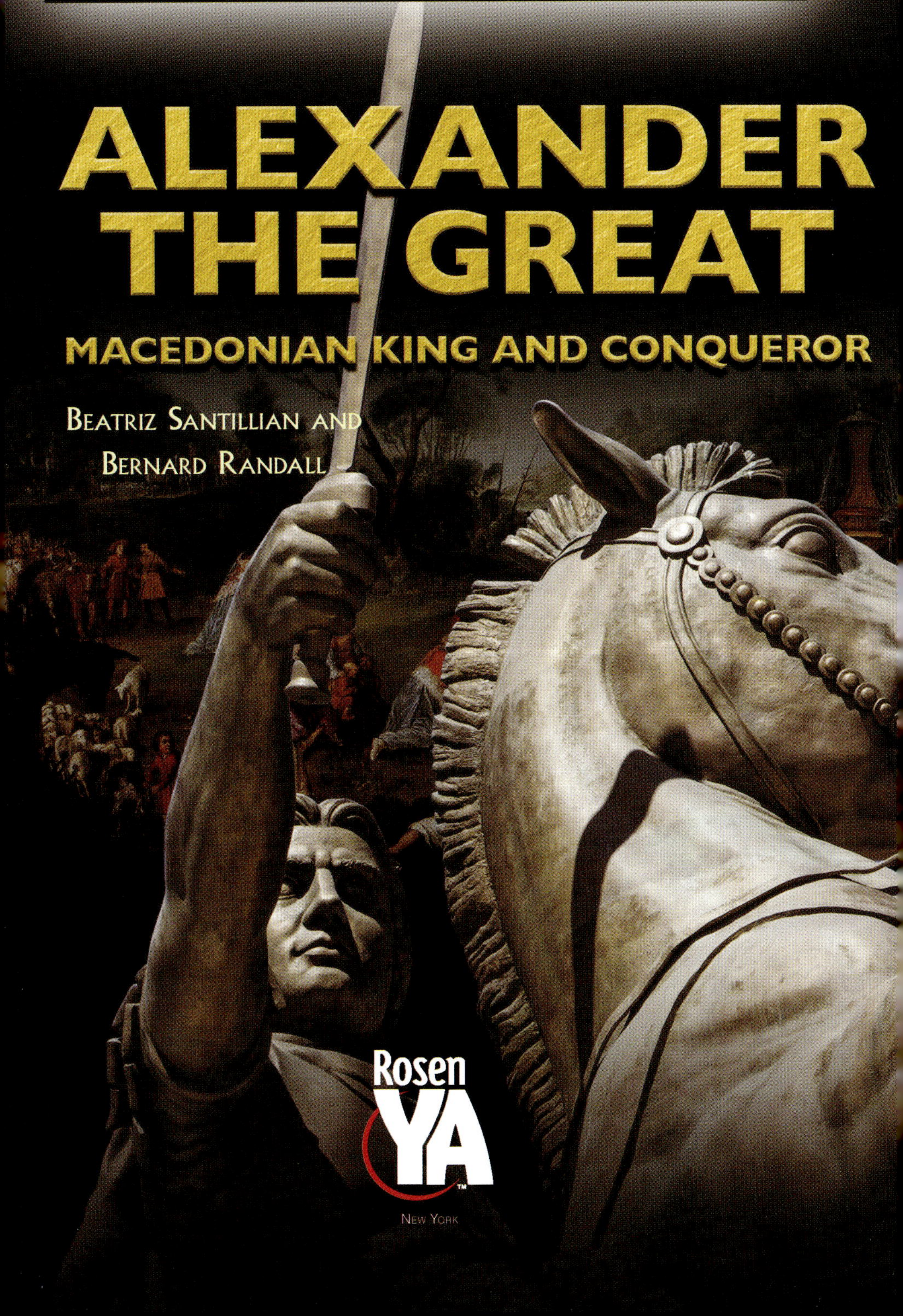

Rosen YA
New York

Published in 2018 by The Rosen Publishing Group, Inc.
29 East 21st Street, New York, NY 10010

First Edition

Library of Congress Cataloging-in-Publication Data

Names: Santillian, Beatriz, author. | Randall, Bernard, author.
Title: Alexander the Great : Macedonian king and conqueror / Beatriz Santillian and Bernard Randall.
Description: First Edition. | New York : Rosen Publishing, 2018. | Series: Leaders of the ancient world | Includes bibliographical references and index. | Audience: Grades 7–12.
Identifiers: LCCN 2016053651 | ISBN 9781508174820 (library bound)
Subjects: LCSH: Alexander, the Great, 356 B.C.–323 B.C—Juvenile literature. | Greece—History—Macedonian Expansion, 359–323 B.C—Juvenile literature. | Generals—Greece—Biography—Juvenile literature. | Greece—Kings and rulers—Biography—Juvenile literature.
Classification: LCC DF234 .S157 2016 | DDC 938/.07092 [B] —dc23
LC record available at https://lccn.loc.gov/2016053651

Manufactured in China

On the cover: *Foreground*: Statue of Alexander the Great on Bucephalus in Skopje Square, Macedonia. *Background*: 1630 Esaias van de Velde painting of Alexander the Great and his captives, the family of King Darius III.

CONTENTS

INTRODUCTION

Alexander the Great: his name fit the values of his time, when the world was full of ambitious, would-be leaders who wanted to wage glorious wars to expand their territory, a time when the death of a king meant a bloody power struggle between factions that would drastically change the lives of the people who were ruled. Such was the environment in which he grew up and rose to power.

King Alexander III of Macedon (where Greece is now) lived from 356 to 323 BCE. In that time, he was able to rely on the power and confidence of his army to keep Macedon safe. And so much more! Alexander forged the biggest empire in the world after securing his place as leader in 336 BCE. Between years of trying to overcome his opponents and build a secure domain, he masterfully established a strong, if not always agreeable rulership in places

Pictured (*above*) is King Darius III of the Persian Empire, mortal enemy of Alexander the Great.

that he conquered, maintained the morale of his troops, and adjusted to some particularly challenging circumstances to allow for military success.

But the impact of his campaigns goes far beyond the fighting that occurred. Amidst slaughtering those who resisted and dominating just about everyone he encountered, Alexander, unlike some of his troops, acknowledged the value of the cultures he encountered just as quickly as he acknowledged the financial gain that their conquest brought to his empire. Naturally, as a result he was directly involved in the spread of cultures around the empire, and ultimately, around the world.

The history of Alexander is derived from Greek, Roman, and Oriental texts, all secondary sources. But there are various challenges that come with relying on these sources. Texts may suffer from the biases of its authors. Authors from various traditions may offer a different account of the same event. Limited perspectives also produce different accounts.

Naturally, any text that must be translated may lose some of its meaning in the process, as differences in language may not be reconcilable, or even correctly determined. And the way we interpret the value and meaning of history today may offer a different sentiment than the consensus of that era.

An even more limiting issue is how modern laws impact the ability to seek out information. Depending on the country, an active copyright may protect (or prevent) open access to a sufficiently modified text, such as a translation. This may create a need for a new translation, and this can also cause a disagreement in what the original text or the old translation means. And, the sacredness (religious or secular) of a land's artifacts may, in itself, be deemed reason enough not to remove it from a country.

These were the types of issues that need to be accounted for in writing this book. We have offered multiple perspectives where more than one account existed, and analysis that attempted to understand Alexander's thought process when faced with certain problems. We tried to understand not only Alexander, but his friends, his army, and his enemies. As with all things past, we cannot be sure what happened, but we can be confident in our ability to be objective and honest.

CHAPTER 1

ON THE HEELS OF HIS FATHER

In his youth, Alexander would quickly learn that his people, the Macedonians, were all about waging wars of conquest. The circumstances of his upbringing make it easy to understand how he was well prepared to take on the role of emperor.

HIS LEGENDARY LINEAGE

Alexander was born in the summer of 356 BCE, probably around July 20. His father was King Philip II of Macedon and his mother was Olympias, a princess from a neighboring kingdom.

Olympias was a major influence on Alexander. Philip was away fighting his wars for long periods of Alexander's childhood, and he also had other wives. Any son of the king might inherit the throne, and so Olympias guarded Alexander jealously. But despite his mother's concerns for her son, Alexander's position as the heir to the Macedonian throne was secure, and his father's affection for him was never in doubt.

When Alexander was about twelve, Philip was given a fine black stallion named Bucephalus, which means "ox-head," but it seemed too wild and no one in the king's court was able to

Alexander rides Bucephalus after discovering why he is such an unruly horse.

ride it. Just as the royal party was about to give up, Alexander said that he would tame the horse. He had noticed that Bucephalus was startled by its own shadow. Alexander turned Bucephalus to face the sun so that it could no longer see its shadow, calmed it down, and succeeded in riding it. Bucephalus became Alexander's favorite horse, and he would later ride it in battle. This and other examples of Alexander's boldness and wiliness only increased Philip's pride and affection for his son.

GREECE AND MACEDON

Alexander's father, Philip, encouraged the influence of Greek culture in Macedon. Greek became the official language of the army and the government administration. Philip appointed Aristotle, the famous Greek philosopher, as Alexander's tutor between the ages of thirteen and sixteen. Aristotle's interests were encyclopedic, from philosophy and art to politics and science. It is clear that Alexander learned a lot from Aristotle, and when he invaded the Persian Empire, he took philosophers and scientists with him.

But the fact that Philip admired Greek culture did not prevent him from coveting their lands and cities. After consolidating his power in Macedon and securing the borders, Philip turned his attention to Greece. In 340 BCE, Philip went to war against some Greeks living on the border of Macedon, and left Alexander, only sixteen at the time, in charge at home. While Philip was away, a small tribe in northern Macedon revolted, and Alexander took control of the effort to suppress the rebellion. The following year Alexander accompanied his father on a major campaign into the lands north of Macedon.

It was in 338 BCE that Alexander got his first taste of battle. Philip had invaded Greece, and at Chaeronea the Macedonians met the army of an alliance of Greek states. Alexander was put in command of the cavalry, the most important part of the army. Philip's battle plan was superb, and Alexander played his part perfectly. The Macedonian victory was complete. The Greeks had little option but to submit to Philip, and he forced them to sign a treaty bringing them together in an organization known as the League of Corinth. Philip got himself elected president of the League and supreme general for the war he now planned to wage against the Persian Empire.

MILITARY STRATEGY

Philip had remodeled the Macedonian army so that it became the most efficient fighting force of the time. The element of the army that made it so effective was the cavalry. Because stirrups had not yet been invented, men on horseback lacked the proper support for wielding heavy swords or accurately aiming bows. Therefore, most cavalry units were armed with lances or javelins. They would ride to within range of the enemy, throw their weapons, and then gallop away before the enemy could catch them. The job of the cavalry was to harass and weaken enemy infantry, but in a frontal assault they could not be expected to break a unit of infantry if the foot soldiers kept their discipline and stood firm. Using their javelins as thrusting weapons, cavalry units could fight other mounted soldiers in hand-to-hand combat, but the infantry carried out most of the serious fighting.

Philip decided to make broader use of the Macedonian cavalry and to take advantage of

These are Macedonian phalanx soldiers. When fighting, they hold their shields on their left, and their weapons on their right.

their superior mobility. He trained his mounted troops to be superb horsemen who could control their horses and, most importantly, stay on them when fighting in close quarters. It was customary for units of infantry of this period to deploy in a dense rectangular block of men all facing the same way. This was called a phalanx. Effective as such a

THE PHALANX EVOLVES

King Phillip wasn't the first to employ or modify the phalanx. Its earliest use has been dated back to the Sumerians during the 25th century BCE, and it has seen continued use in ancient Egypt and the many states of Greece.

The evolution of this fighting style was one of necessity. A simple phalanx consists of a group of men standing behind their shields in close quarters in a horizontal line, offering their group collective protection. Instead of the usual even horizontal alignment, Miltiades secured the victory of his forces during the battle of Marathon in 490 BCE by distributing his troops in greater numbers on the wings, leaving the center less covered.

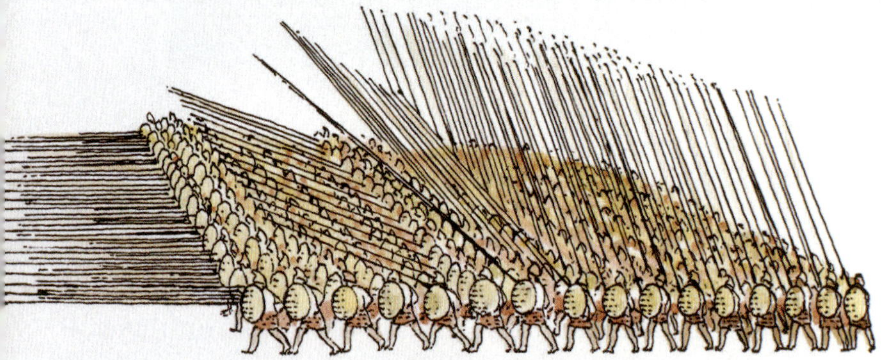

This illustration depicts the phalanx formation of Alexander the Great's infantry.

Another winning strategy occurred in 371 BCE. Theban general Epaminondas put his soldiers in a diagonal formation, called the oblique phalanx. This allowed for a more focused attack on an area of the battlefield—specifically, the area where troops were placed closer to the enemy.

unit was, Philip realized that it was vulnerable if a highly mobile cavalry could outflank the phalanx and attack its side or rear.

It became the role of the Macedonian infantry to hold the enemy infantry in place long enough for the cavalry to ride around behind them. In order to do this, the infantry units formed a phalanx at least eight men deep, but sometimes there were as many as sixteen or thirty-two ranks of soldiers in the phalanx. The Macedonians used lances or pikes eighteen feet or more in length. This meant that at least four spear-points would protrude in front of the man in the front rank, each carried by a man behind him, making it much harder to break through the line. The Macedonian phalanx presented to the enemy a dense, porcupine-like mass of spears. By weight of numbers the phalanx would either hold the enemy in place or slowly push them back. The key to this style of fighting was teamwork, and Philip made sure that his men were highly trained.

There were many other troops in the Macedonian army. Each nationality or group under Macedonian control had its own style of fighting. This variety was another source of strength, because it meant that whatever the terrain and whatever the task, there were troops who could get the job done. But the coordinated use of infantry and cavalry and the tactics of pinning down enemy units and then outflanking or encircling them were innovations that would serve well an army on the offensive, and that would create the foundation for a new type of mobile warfare.

Having gained control of Greece, Philip turned his attention to Asia.

CLAIMING THE THRONE

In 336 BCE, Philip took time out from preparing his army to celebrate the marriage of his daughter Cleopatra to his brother-in-law Alexander, king of Epirus, a region on the border of Macedon. Alexander of Epirus was the brother of Olympias, Alexander's mother, and Cleopatra was her daughter. Phillip invited special guests and dignitaries from all over Hellas. After the marriage ceremony, Philip walked into the theater for the celebrations, leaving his guards at a distance to show his confidence in the goodwill of his guests. One of his bodyguards, called Pausanias, rushed forward, pulled out a concealed dagger, and fatally stabbed Philip. Pausanias ran for a horse he had placed nearby, but he tripped and was killed by the other bodyguards.

Pausanias assassinates King Philip by stabbing him to death.

The throne was now empty, and Philip's leading generals quickly declared their support for Alexander. This was partly because it had been clear that Philip wanted him as his heir, and partly because of genuine regard for the young prince. The army installed Alexander as king at the age of twenty.

Alexander had to deal with two problems before his grip on the throne became secure. His cousin Amyntas was also a serious candidate for the kingship. Amyntas was easily dealt with, however. Early in 335 BCE he was accused of treason for plotting against Alexander and executed. Whether he was in fact guilty is not known, but it was commonly the case that rivals for the throne were eliminated by whatever means were easiest.

More serious for Alexander was the suggestion that he had been involved in the murder of his father. If this charge was proved the army might turn against him, because Philip had been very popular. The person who had benefited most from Philip's death was, of course, Alexander, and there had been a very public rift between him and his father:

In 337 BCE Philip had married his sixth wife, Cleopatra, the niece and ward of one of his leading *hetairoi*, Attalus. Philip's other wives were now too old to have children, and he only had two sons, Alexander and Philip Arrhidaeus. Philip Arrhidaeus suffered learning difficulties, so the king wanted to make sure that there would be a fit heir to succeed him in case anything happened to Alexander. It seems that Olympias was jealous of this new and much younger wife. To make matters worse, Cleopatra was of Macedonian ancestry, whereas Olympias was a foreigner. At a drunken party, it was said, Attalus provoked Alexander by claiming that his niece would provide a pure-blooded Macedonian heir to the throne. Alexander threw his drink at Attalus, which enraged Philip so much that he drew his sword to attack Alexander. Fortunately for his son, Philip was so drunk that he tripped and fell, prompting Alexander to comment that the man who wished to cross from Europe into Asia could not cross from one chair to another. Whether or not the story is true, for some reason Alexander, most of his closest friends, and his mother Olympias went into temporary exile. They were soon recalled, however, and Alexander was back in favor at the time of Philip's murder.

It is believed that Pausanias acted alone in killing Philip, and that his motive had been an incident with Attalus's servants. These servants had apparently assaulted him, and Philip had refused to punish Attalus. It is unlikely that Alexander was involved in the murder of his father, since that would have been the most religiously and morally outrageous act he could commit, and Alexander was devoutly religious. However, it is possible that Olympias had encouraged some kind of plot against Philip because of her jealousy over Cleopatra. Pausanias's death before being questioned is also a source of skepticism of the idea that he worked alone, since he was quickly silenced. Whatever the truth of the matter, Alexander arranged for a grand funeral for Philip. In a purge both of Alexander's personal enemies and those suspected of treason against Philip, Attalus was killed and his niece Cleopatra was also eliminated, allegedly murdered by Olympias herself. The tomb of Philip has been found by archaeologists, and one of his wives is buried with him, almost certainly Cleopatra. By giving Cleopatra the burial of a queen, Alexander showed that he held no grudge, thus removing any lingering suspicions over the death of Philip.

CHAPTER 2

ALEXANDER AT WAR

It wasn't long before word of the king's passing spread around the areas he had invaded. What Alexander did next set the stage for determining what kind of ruler he would be, and his father's influence would be clear throughout his every move.

RECLAIMING GREECE

Having come to the throne, Alexander intended to carry out the invasion of Asia that his father had planned. However, he had to secure his own position first. The Greeks had never been happy to be ruled from Macedon, and they threatened to revolt. But Alexander, with the swiftness that was to become characteristic of him, marched south so quickly that there was no time for the Greeks to organize any resistance. The Greeks had no option but to recognize the strength of Alexander's position and declare him president of the League of Corinth and supreme general, like his father before him.

The following year, Alexander took his army north to make sure that the borders of Macedon would not be threatened while he was away. In a successful campaign he extended the Macedonian frontier to the Danube River. While he was away there was a revolt in Greece, centered in the city of Thebes. Marching back into Greece, Alexander attacked Thebes and, in the massacre that followed, his army killed one-sixth of the population. The remaining inhabitants, some 30,000 men, women, and children, were sold into slavery. With his position at home secure, Alexander was now ready to invade Asia. He appointed as his deputy Antipater, one his father's ablest and most trusted generals. Antipater was to stay behind, watch over Macedon and Greece, and arrange for reinforcements to be sent out to Alexander when they were needed.

TURNING TOWARD ASIA MINOR

At the time when Alexander decided to invade the Persian Empire, it covered almost the entire known world east of Macedon—modern Turkey, Syria, Lebanon, Jordan, Israel, Egypt, Iraq, Kuwait, Iran, and Afghanistan. The Persian Empire had been founded by Cyrus the Great in 549 BCE when he usurped the throne of the empire of the Medes, who had themselves overrun the Assyrian empire, and began to extend its dominion over other peoples. A succession of empires had dominated the whole of the Middle East for centuries. However, the most successful empires were the ones that allowed local peoples to enjoy their own cultures without interference.

Artexerxes III was king of the Persian Empire and an absolute monarch until his death in 338 BCE. However, the rule of Cyrus the Great, the founder of the Persian Empire, was governed by principles of compassion. The reign of Darius III, who eventually followed Artexerxes III, was considered mild and forgiving. He ruled his empire through a system of local governors, known as *satraps*, who administered

The green portion of this map shows the extent of the Persian Empire, which began in 549 BCE.

various geographical areas on his behalf. As long as the satraps sent the required amount of taxes and tribute to the capital, they were left to govern as they wished. There was also a fairly efficient secret service. Its main

job was to keep watch over the satraps and other administrators to ensure that they did not plan a revolt.

At the start of the fifth century BCE the Persians had attacked Greece, but only with limited success. In 490 BCE the army of Darius I was defeated at Marathon. In 480 BCE another army under Xerxes captured Athens and destroyed most of its temples. An alliance of Greek states drove the Persians out, but the Greeks never forgot what happened. When Philip decided to try to unite the Greeks—under his own leadership, of course—he used the excuse of the need to wage a war to punish the Persians. Alexander would undertake this war with spectacular results. After the successes of Philip it must have seemed natural to Alexander to want to extend Macedonian power, and the wealth of the Persian Empire must have been another irresistible incentive.

The two ancient Greek warriors pictured here are fighting each other as part of their training to become a part of the infantry.

RITUALS OF WAR

Early in the spring of 334 BCE Alexander crossed into Asia at the head of his army. He had with him a force of around 32,000 infantry and 5,100 cavalry. Of the infantry, 12,000 were Macedonian pikemen, and an equal number were Greek infantrymen. Most of the remaining 8,000 infantry were archers. There were 1,800 Macedonian cavalry. The rest of the cavalry were from the Macedonian territories. Although the Macedonians were the elite forces, the whole army was well trained and well equipped. Alexander also had with him a number of experienced hetairoi, especially Parmenio.

The first thing that Alexander did was to visit the city of Troy in the northwestern corner of modern Turkey. This was the site of the exploits of his supposed ancestor Achilles in the war of the Greeks against the Trojans. Alexander liked to compare himself to Achilles. It was said that Alexander slept with a copy of *The Iliad* under his pillow every night to remind him of what Achilles had done. At Troy, Alexander placed a wreath at the grave of Achilles, and his closest friend, Hephaestion, did the same at the tomb of Patroclus, who had been Achilles's closest friend and lover.

Alexander also sacrificed to the goddess Athena and dedicated his armor to her, leaving it in her temple. He received in return a shield that was supposed to have been left from the time of the Trojan War. If genuine, this shield would have been around eight hundred years old. Alexander had it carried into battle with him.

IN PURSUIT OF THE PERSIAN EMPIRE

Darius III, the king of the Persian Empire, obviously did not feel very threatened by Alexander's invasion, for he left the defense of his territories to the local satraps. Alexander marched east with all his cavalry and the Macedonian infantry. At the Granicus River (the modern-day Kocabas), he encountered a Persian army.

According to Arrian, there were 20,000 Persian cavalry and an equal number of Greek mercenaries in the Persian army. They had taken up a position on the far side of the Granicus, with the cavalry in a line

DESCENDANCY AND RELIGION

The claim was often made that a ruler had descended directly from gods. In the case of Alexander the Great, his initial claims to divine relation were Achilles, the son of a water nymph named Thetis, and Heracles, son of Zeus. As he progressed in conquering various lands, Alexander took on other divine titles. The priest of Amun described him as the son of Amun after conquering Egypt, and he himself took on the title of son of Zeus beyond the domain of Egypt sometime afterward.

But being a god isn't everything. It was common—certainly, expected—for rulers to demonstrate the depths of their beliefs by offering sacrifices. After all, they thought that their level of favor with the gods was the single most important determining factor of success.

in front and the Greek infantry behind. The river was fast-flowing and had steep banks—five yards high in some places. It looked impossible for the Macedonians, outnumbered as they were, to force their way across the river. Alexander nevertheless gave the order to attack, against the advice of Parmenio. He stationed most of the cavalry on the right, with himself in overall command. The phalanx of Macedonians was on the left, under the command of Parmenio.

One unit of Macedonian cavalry, whose commander was named Socrates, engaged the line of Persian cavalry while the rest of the Macedonian horsemen under Alexander carefully crossed the river. The Persians met Socrates's squadron with their best men, causing a number of casualties. At this point Alexander observed a small gap in the Persian line. He charged into it at the head of his best cavalry. Alexander himself was the first to reach the top of the riverbank and the level ground above it. This was a dangerous moment for Alexander. The white plumes on his helmet were easily recognizable, and an elite unit of the Persian cavalry made straight for him. Alexander unseated their commander, Mithridates, a son-in-law of the Persian king, but then a Persian called Rhoesaces swung at him and cut off part of his helmet. Alexander ran Rhoesaces through with his lance, but now he was exposed, and Rhoesaces's brother, Spithridates, raised his sword to deliver a fatal blow. Just at that moment Cleitus, one of Alexander's bodyguards, struck Spithridates so hard that he cut off his whole arm. Alexander was saved, but it had been a close call. By now, more of the Macedonians were reaching the top of the riverbank, and the infantry phalanx had begun to cross as well. Persian javelins were no match for the longer lances and pikes of the Macedonians, and the Persian cavalry soon turned and fled, leaving the

This 1665 CE painting by Charles Le Brun depicts the Battle of the Granicus River.

Greek mercenaries behind them totally exposed. Surrounded, the Greeks were massacred. Only two thousand out of twenty thousand were taken prisoner, to be sent as slaves to Macedon.

ADVANCING THROUGH ASIA MINOR

Alexander's first battle in Persian territory had nearly been his last, but he had won it through his own leadership. Although the Persian commanders had made mistakes, such as forming two separate battle lines of cavalry and infantry so that only one could fight at a time, a less able general might not have managed to exploit these mistakes. With the Persians defeated, Alexander was able to take control of Asia Minor. There was little resistance as he marched south. Greeks inhabited most of these areas near the Aegean Sea, and they must have preferred to be ruled by a Macedonian rather than by Persians. Indeed, Alexander became popular amongst them, often excusing them from taxation. For the inhabitants of the non-Greek cities in the region, it was more a case of exchanging one ruler for another, with the same taxes to pay. Alexander was forced to besiege Miletus and

Halicarnassus, two cities that refused to submit, but otherwise he simply stationed garrisons at key points to keep control over his newly conquered territory.

At the end of 334 BCE, Alexander sent home for the winter any of his soldiers who had married immediately before the start of his invasion. This only increased his already immense popularity with the army. At the same time he continued to march through Asia Minor with the remainder of his army. He established secure lines of supply that enabled him to carry on campaigning throughout the winter, something that was almost unheard of in the ancient world. By the start of 333 BCE the whole southern and western coasts and much of the interior of Asia Minor were under Alexander's control. Alexander wanted to deprive the Persian fleet of safe ports in the eastern Mediterranean, since this would pose a real threat to his control of Greece. Although the Persian fleet had almost complete control of the seas, overall it proved unimportant in the coming war. To keep control of the Persian Empire, Darius would make his main efforts on land.

In the spring of 333 BCE Alexander's army reassembled with reinforcements at Gordium in what is now central Turkey, ready to march further into the Persian Empire. While there, Alexander went to visit the famous oxcart of the legendary King Gordius. The yoke for the oxen had been tied to a pole with a knot so complicated that it was impossible to see the ends. According to the legend, whoever managed to untie the Gordian knot would become king of Asia. Alexander tried to untie the knot, but had no success, so he pulled the pole out of the knot instead. According to some accounts, he actually drew his sword and cut the knot. Alexander then declared that he would fulfill the legendary prophecy. We cannot know whether he believed this himself—after all, he had cheated—but it was certainly a great publicity stunt.

Alexander cuts the Gordian knot as a demonstration of his ability to fulfill the prophesy about the next king of Asia.

CHAPTER 3

ASIA MINOR FALLS

The more Alexander campaigned, the more his reputation preceded him, and to his advantage. Even when that was not enough, the brute force of his army and intelligence of his strategy continued to deliver the results he wanted. But in the wake of relentless war, a deadly weakness would show itself.

DANGEROUS MISFORTUNES

From Gordium, Alexander marched through Asia Minor without resistance as far as the Cilician Gates, a narrow mountain pass. Here the road was so narrow that a fully laden camel could not pass along it. If the defenders had stood firm it would have been impossible for Alexander to force his way through. Fortunately for the Macedonians, the Persians fled as soon as Alexander approached. His reputation was working in his favor. The way now lay open to the prosperous city of Tarsus and the road down the coast to what are now Lebanon and Israel. The local satrap had no hope of stopping Alexander, so he planned to plunder Tarsus before leaving. When Alexander heard of this, he galloped ahead of the army with a small force of cavalry. He covered nearly sixty miles in one day and managed to reach the city in time to save it.

Hot from the ride, Alexander jumped into the icy cold waters of the Cydnus River. Whether because of this, or because of fatigue, Alexander developed a serious fever, and his doctors feared for his life. One of his doctors, a friend since boyhood called Philip, produced a potion that he said would cure Alexander. Just as Alexander was about to drink it, a message arrived from Parmenio, warning him that Philip had been bribed by Darius III to poison him. Alexander simply handed the message to Philip and drank the potion, demonstrating his trust in his friends and his lack of fear in the face of danger.

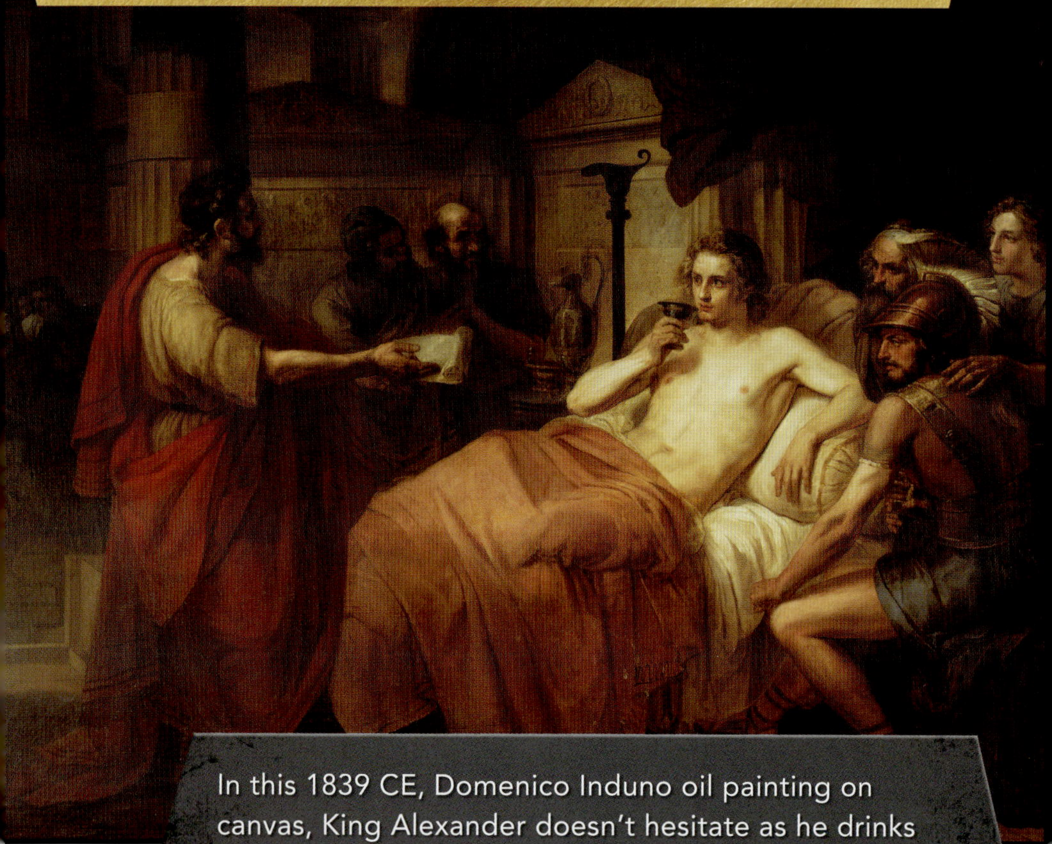

In this 1839 CE, Domenico Induno oil painting on canvas, King Alexander doesn't hesitate as he drinks the medicine his physician Philip has given him.

Alexander had reached Tarsus in the summer of 333 BCE, and it was not until mid October that he recovered completely from his illness. In the meantime, he sent Parmenio out to deal with any Persian forces in the immediate area and to consolidate his supply lines. When news reached Alexander that Darius had assembled an army at Sochi in Syria, he marched south to meet him. Having met up with Parmenio, Alexander left most of his sick and wounded soldiers and his heavy siege equipment at Issus and pressed forward to force a battle.

After two days' march, Alexander discovered that he had made a serious miscalculation. While he had been heading south on the western side of a long mountain range, Darius had been marching north on the eastern side. The Persians had gotten behind Alexander. They captured, mutilated, and killed the Macedonians who had been left at Issus. Then he waited for Alexander to arrive. The situation looked bleak for Alexander. His supply lines had been cut, so he had to fight or starve. Yet Darius had a much bigger army in a good defensive position.

FACE-OFF WITH THE PERSIAN ARMY

However, when Alexander arrived at the Pinarus River, behind which stood the Persian army, he saw that the situation was not as bad as it might have been. Between the sea and the mountains there was a coastal plain a little less than two miles wide, which meant that the Persians did not have enough room for all of their troops to deploy. Nevertheless, the riverbanks were steep in places and would be difficult to climb. Boulders in the riverbed meant that horses trying to charge across it would be in danger of breaking their legs, so it would be up to the infantry to make the first attack.

Alexander put the Macedonian cavalry on the right and placed Parmenio in command of the remaining allied cavalry on the left. In the center was the infantry phalanx, with Alexander commanding the right wing. In all, Alexander had around 5,300 cavalry and 24,000 infantry. Darius is reported to have had 30,000 cavalry, an infantry force of 30,000 Greek mercenaries, and an additional 60,000 Persian infantry. Alexander was very heavily outnumbered. Darius put the majority of his cavalry on his right, facing Parmenio, with the intention of sweeping along the flat shoreline and breaking through to attack the left wing of the infantry phalanx. Darius himself took up a position in the center with his cavalry guards, behind the Greek mercenaries. On the left he placed some cavalry. Parmenio's job was crucial. He had to hold back the massed Persian cavalry long enough for the Macedonian right wing to break through the Persians in front of them.

This 1529 Albrecht Altdorfer painting depicts the massive clash of Macedonian and Persian Empire forces during the battle at Issus in 330 BCE.

On each side, the right wing took the initiative. The Persian cavalry put Parmenio under intense pressure, but because of the limited space they could not make full use of their superior numbers. Alexander led his men across the river at a charge, and they succeeded in breaking through the Persian infantry. To his right, the Macedonian cavalry crossed the river, engaged the Persian cavalry to their front, and drove them back. The whole of the Persian left now collapsed. Joining his cavalry, Alexander charged left toward Darius, who turned and fled. Instead of pursuing him, Alexander carried on toward Parmenio's wing, where the massed Persian cavalry, realizing that Darius had fled and that they were themselves in danger of being surrounded,

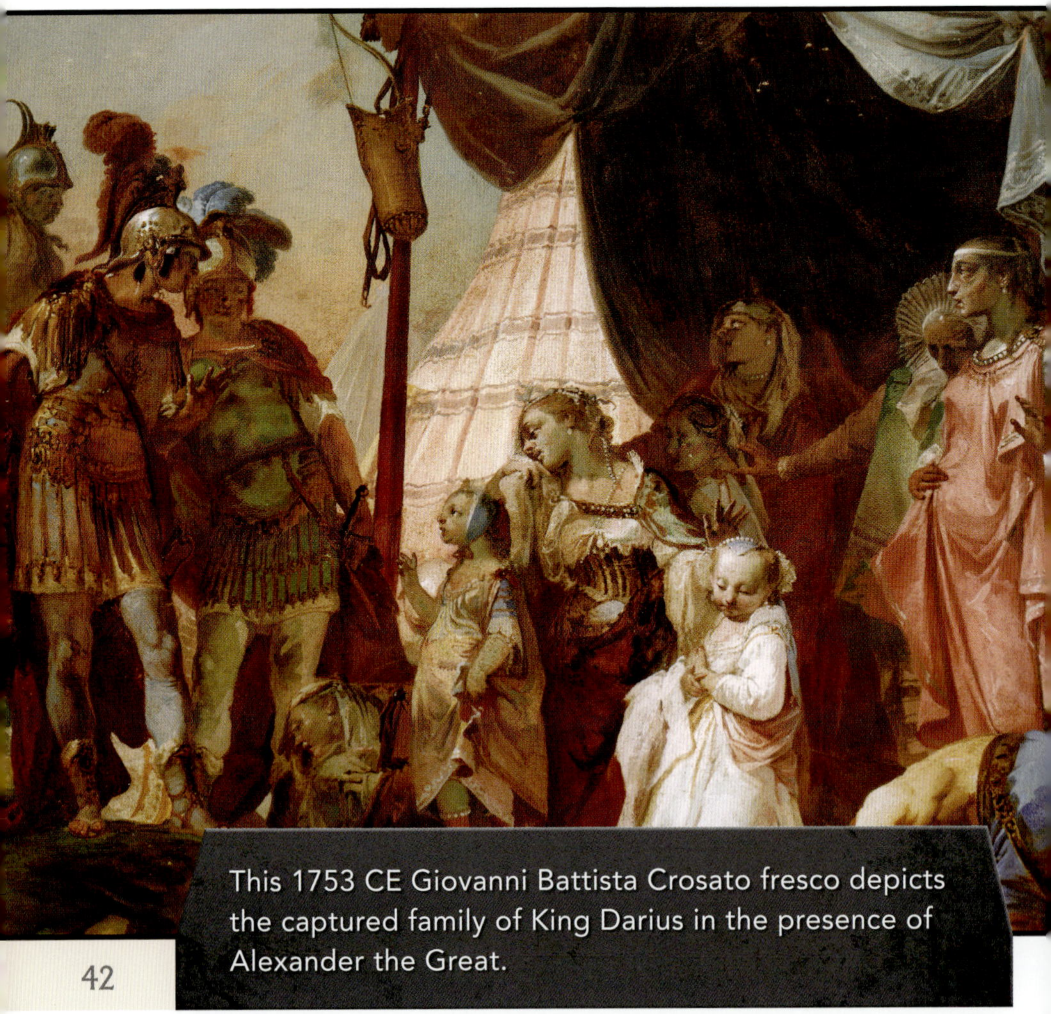

This 1753 CE Giovanni Battista Crosato fresco depicts the captured family of King Darius in the presence of Alexander the Great.

also turned to flee. In the limited space the vast numbers of Persian soldiers got in each other's way and were easy targets. The Macedonian victory was absolute. Although Alexander continued the pursuit until nightfall, Darius escaped into the mountains.

Again, poor tactics on the part of the Persians had helped Alexander, but he could not have won without the discipline and courage of his troops. In particular, Parmenio's leadership of the left wing must have been outstanding for his cavalry to have held out against such an overwhelming force. Alexander himself was an inspired leader, always in front of his troops and always setting an example of bravery for his men to follow.

After the battle Alexander captured Darius's wife and children, who had been left behind in the Persian camp. They were valuable hostages, but Alexander treated them with great respect, as befitted members of a royal family. He assured them that Darius had not been killed, as they had supposed. Alexander also visited the wounded and presided over a grand funeral for the fallen.

ANCIENT HOSTAGES

One common part of war was the taking of particularly advantageous hostages. Not much is known about Alexander's father's time as a hostage, other than that being one gave him the opportunity to observe the military techniques of the Greeks at Thebes. As a royal hostage, he was privileged enough not to be sold as a slave, but really, anything could happen to a captive of war.

It is clear from Alexander's campaigns that the amount of fighting and effort that his army required to complete a conquest had some influence on whether to kill or take potential hostages once a battle was won. In other words, if winning was quick and easy, he was more willing to take prisoners. It may be that Alexander was so kind to some hostages, especially of the royal variety, because of his father's having been in that position. Or perhaps his religious belief in the sanctity of royal status motivated his favorable treatment of some, including the family of his mortal enemy Darius III.

TAKING ON TYRE'S RESISTANCE

Given the chance to march east into Persia itself, Alexander wisely chose to first consolidate his position by heading south along the Mediterranean coast as far as Egypt. Persia could wait, but the enemy fleet was still active in the Aegean Sea. Many of the Persians' ships came from ports along the coast, and if their homelands were captured the Persians would lose their services. By taking control of the entire eastern Mediterranean, Alexander could completely deprive the Persian fleet of bases and finally take it out of the picture.

As Alexander marched south the cities he came to all submitted without resistance. Except for Tyre. The inhabitants sent ambassadors offering to obey his orders. Alexander said that he wished to sacrifice to their chief god Melkart. This was something only the king of Tyre was permitted to do, and so they refused him. Alexander decided to besiege Tyre. The task seemed impossible, which is why the Tyrians felt safe in defying Alexander. Their city lay on an island half a mile offshore and was protected by 150-foot-high walls. They had plenty of food and other supplies. They expected assistance from the Persian fleet, and they had their own small fleet that commanded the sea around the island.

Alexander ordered his men to build a 200-foot-wide causeway from the mainland to the island. As this causeway approached the island the water got deeper, and the Tyrians used catapults to make the work impossible. The Macedonians built two 150-foot-high wooden towers and placed their own catapults on them. These were reported to be the highest siege towers ever used in the ancient world. They were dragged to the end of the causeway, where the Macedonians kept up a covering fire on the walls of Tyre, and the construction work continued. In a daring response, the Tyrians towed a ship to the end of the causeway and set it on fire, burning all the Macedonians' equipment and destroying the towers.

FINISHING AT TYRE

Alexander now began to make the causeway wider, and he brought up naval ships from the port cities that had surrendered to him. He now had more ships than the Tyrians, assembled from the very fleet that the Tyrians had expected to rescue them. The Tyrians blocked their own harbor and continued to resist.

Alexander tried siege weapons from his ships. The Tyrians swam underwater to cut the anchor ropes, until these were replaced with chains. The Tyrians lowered padding over the walls to protect them from catapults, and threw huge boulders into the sea to prevent Alexander's ships from getting close to the wall. But whatever the Tyrians tried, there was no escape. Although unable to break through the wall at the causeway, Alexander's battering rams eventually broke through on the south side of the island. Bringing up two naval ships full of Macedonian infantry, Alexander was again in the thick of the fighting as his men forced their way into the city. At the same time, his fleet finally breached the harbor defenses. The Tyrians were slaughtered. The siege had taken seven

King Alexander the Great's forces battle it out during the siege of Tyre. Tyre was an unfortunate one of few cities that resisted the Macedonian ruler's army.

months, and the Macedonians were eager to dominate. The survivors, around 30,000 of them, were sold into slavery, and Alexander made lavish sacrifices to Melkart. The causeway Alexander constructed still exists as part of an isthmus linking Tyre to the mainland.

Tyre fell in July 332 BCE, and around this time the Persian king Darius offered a peace proposal to Alexander. Darius offered a huge ransom for the return of his wife and children. He promised Alexander his daughter's hand in marriage, and he offered to surrender all his land east of the Euphrates River in exchange for a treaty of peace and friendship. The story is that Parmenio told Alexander that he would accept these terms and end the war if he were Alexander. Alexander replied that if he were Parmenio he would accept, but since he was Alexander he would not. Alexander's decision was perfectly reasonable. Darius was offering him little more territory than he already had taken, and certainly much less than he hoped to acquire.

CHAPTER 4

CONQUERING EGYPT

Alexander's blood constantly raged with a lust for war. Whether he was motivated by his father's unfinished dream of taking on the Persian Empire, his own frustration from failing to achieve absolute victory against Darius III, or simply the desire to improve the wealth of his domain, his speed and his persistence tell a tale of a man who would not be stopped.

CLAIMING THE RICHES OF THE MEDITERRANEAN

After taking Tyre, Alexander continued south, meeting resistance only at Gaza. There was another siege, and Alexander was badly injured by a catapult bolt that went through his shield and pierced his shoulder. Gaza was taken only when the siege engines that had been used at Tyre were brought down the coast.

From Gaza to Egypt, Alexander had to cross 140 miles of the Sinai desert. As always, he took great care to make sure that his troops were properly supplied. The army followed a route along the coast, with the fleet carrying the heavy equipment and large supplies of fresh water. When he arrived in Egypt Alexander met no resistance, for the Egyptians themselves had a history of opposing Persian rule. Alexander was proclaimed the new pharaoh, and he sacrificed to the Egyptian gods.

And so, at the end of 332 BCE, Alexander was ruler of all the eastern coasts of the Mediterranean, including the richest country of all in the Mediterranean, Egypt. The Persian fleet had nowhere to go and could no longer threaten the Macedonian forces. Alexander could now look east to Persia itself. But before continuing with his conquests there were two things that he wanted to do. The first was to found a new city.

Alexander founded many cities in the course of his campaigns. Many of them were small places, just large enough to support a garrison and keep his lines of supply open. In these cities he would

In this halftone illustration, Alexander the Great's forces lay siege to Gaza. The same siege engines that penetrated Tyre conquered Gaza.

often settle mercenaries who had come to the end of their contracts, or troops who had suffered injuries bad enough to prevent them from fighting in battle. Sometimes the aim of the city was to bring the native people of an area closer to civilization, giving them access to marketplaces and cultural benefits, and giving tax collectors access to them.

This city, however, was different. There was no need to control supply lines, and the locals were already highly civilized. This was to be a great trading port, and the site chosen had two superb natural harbors. Alexander personally marked out the streets and boundaries of the new city, where the temples would be, and which gods would be

The Pharos lighthouse in Alexandria, Egypt. When Alexander the Great founded this city in 332 BCE, he made sure that it was more than just a military stronghold.

THE SEVEN WONDERS OF THE ANCIENT WORLD

As with most of the Seven Wonders of the World, the Pharos lighthouse is no longer standing. This particular wonder was erected well after Alexander's reign, during the 3rd century BCE, and was damaged by earthquakes in 1303 and 1323 CE. It disappeared in 1480 CE when some of its remaining materials were used for Fort Qaitbey.

The others that have been destroyed in various natural disasters or human acts are the Colossus of Rhodes, the Lighthouse of Alexandria, the Mausoleum at Halicarnassus, the Temple of Artemis, and the Statue of Zeus. Only the Great Pyramid of Giza remains intact.

worshiped in them. Alexander named the city Alexandria, after himself. Alexandria was to become for a time the largest city in the ancient world. Alexandria was not only an incredibly wealthy center of trade, it was a center of intellectual and cultural development as well. It had a world-famous library. It was the place where Eratosthenes accurately measured the circumference of the earth. Here Hero invented the steam engine. Here the first book on algebra was written. And here many of the greatest theologians of early Christianity were based. Alexandria is most famous for its Pharos lighthouse, one of the Seven Wonders of the Ancient World.

THE ORACLE

The other thing that Alexander did in Egypt was to visit the renowned oracle of Amun at Siwa with a small group of companions. This involved a 200-mile trek westward along the Mediterranean coast, and then south across the desert for a further 100 miles to the oasis of Siwa. Here was a temple of Amun, where the priest would take on the character of the god and answer questions with nods and gestures. When Alexander's party arrived the priest welcomed the Macedonian king as the son of Amun and led him inside the temple to ask his questions, leaving everyone else outside. When Alexander emerged, he declared that he was happy with the answers he had received, and the party left Siwa.

The Siwa Oasis (*pictured*) was the destination of many who wanted to know the fortunes and fates of the future.

This is one of the most controversial episodes in Alexander's life, for we have no knowledge of what questions Alexander asked or what responses he got to them. Many of those who have written about him have speculated about his questions. Did he ask whether he was immortal? Or did he ask if he would conquer the rest of the Persian Empire? Did he want to know whether all of his father's murderers had been caught? Or was it merely that, as was usual when founding a city, he asked the nearest oracle whether the god looked kindly on the project?

Plutarch, in his biography of Alexander, quoted a letter supposedly written by Alexander to his mother, Olympias, which said that he had received secret replies that he would reveal only to her on his return home. It seems likely that this is genuine, in which case we can be fairly sure that no one else knew exactly what went on in the temple. If he would not tell his mother, he is hardly likely to have told anyone else. The fact that the priest of Amun welcomed Alexander as the son of Amun means little in itself since this was no more than a proper way of greeting the new pharaoh.

Probably even before the visit to Siwa, Alexander came to believe that he was not the same as other men. His great successes on the battlefield confirmed it in his eyes, as his culture attributed success and failure to the will of the gods, and rule was thought of as a divine gift to the direct descendant of a god. We know that Olympias encouraged the young Alexander to model himself on the heroes of Greek mythology, and this sense of greatness would have seemed natural to him since he was supposedly descended from Achilles on his mother's side and Heracles on his father's side.

Later, Alexander would refer to himself as the son of Zeus (he apparently referred to Philip as his "so-called father"). Perhaps because the pharaoh had always been seen as the son of a god, he thought it right that he should be thought of as divine outside Egypt as well. At some point, a story was circulated that Olympias had been impregnated by Zeus in the form of a snake, conceiving Alexander. We cannot know when this story was first put forward, but it was likely spread after Alexander's visit to Siwa. And as a worshiper of Dionysus, Olympias was known to keep snakes, which may have inspired the legend.

DARIUS III RETURNS

In the summer of 331 BCE Alexander learned that Darius had assembled a new army at Babylon. The Macedonian commander returned to Tyre, made sure that everything was in order, and then marched east to meet Darius.

When Alexander reached the Euphrates River (in modern-day Iraq), Darius expected him to march along it toward the city of Babylon. Instead Alexander crossed over and headed for the Tigris River, staying north of Darius. The reason is obvious enough. The wide floodplains

Olympias's worship of Dionysus (*left*) offered a source for rumors about the divine conception of Alexander.

of the Euphrates and Tigris rivers are ideal for cavalry. Since Darius had far more cavalry than Alexander, the Macedonians sought to avoid giving the Persians an advantage. Each king hoped that the other would come to meet him where he wanted to fight. It was Darius who marched to meet Alexander. The fact that Alexander was conquering the territory in the north certainly influenced Darius's decision. Darius also had a far larger army to feed and pay for, and waiting was expensive. Although the terrain east of the Tigris was not suitable for the hit-and-run cavalry tactics that would have given Darius the edge, he managed to find a battlefield near Gaugamela with enough room for his cavalry to maneuver.

Having received reinforcements, Alexander had about 7,000 cavalry and 40,000 infantry at his disposal, including mercenaries. Darius, however, had 35,000 to 40,000 cavalry and huge numbers of infantry. Ancient estimates range from 200,000 to one million men, but even the lower figure is now considered an exaggeration. The Persian horsemen were good soldiers, but most of the infantry were not, and they played little part in the battle.

A COWARD FLEES

On September 30, 331 BCE, Alexander arrived at Gaugamela with his army, and established his camp early enough so that the men were well rested. It seems that Darius kept his men standing in battle positions all night, perhaps fearing a surprise attack. The battle plans were much the same as at Issus. Darius hoped that his cavalry would break through on the right. Alexander was again relying on Parmenio to hold out while he himself tried to break through the Persian lines.

On October 1, Alexander led his men into battle. Unlike at Issus, because of the broad plain there was no protection for the flanks of his army, and the Macedonians were in danger of being surrounded. Alexander cleverly used this to his advantage by advancing diagonally to the right instead of straight ahead. The Persians moved left in response to maintain their overlapping positions and, because they were less disciplined, a gap started to open in the Persian line. Alexander seized his moment and charged into the gap, forcing his way through. Parmenio led the resistance on the left. Alexander made for

Darius's position behind the Persian frontline troops. Darius's soldiers temporarily stopped this daring assault, but Darius had little faith in them, and fled the battlefield.

With their king no longer present, and faced with the threat of Alexander attacking them from behind after a breakthrough, the Persian army

Darius III and his soldiers flee from the battle of Gaugamela.

crumbled. Darius's lack of courage had betrayed him and he retreated before the battle was lost. Once again Alexander had won the day, and this time the heart of the Persian Empire lay open to him. Alexander again had to rely on the courage and discipline of his men. Nevertheless, the crucial factor was his superior generalship. He had devised a plan to win against the odds, and he had put that plan into action.

CHAPTER 5

VICTORY IN PERSIA

Darius III's flight opened the path for Alexander to advance his victory over the Persian Empire. But his victory would be incomplete if Darius could raise another army, as he did in Babylon. Besides that, it was likely that other Persians would oppose his rule if he didn't act to put himself, as opposed to other potential heirs, at the forefront of rule in the Persian Empire.

ALEXANDER'S PERSIAN EMPIRE

For the first time, Alexander had himself publicly proclaimed "king of Asia." When he marched south to Babylon the local satrap surrendered without a fight. The Babylonians had not enjoyed Persian rule because Xerxes, a previous king of the

Persian Empire, had destroyed their main temple as punishment for a revolt. Alexander promised to rebuild that temple. He also reappointed the old satrap, a policy he followed throughout most of his newly conquered territory. None of Alexander's men knew the people of an area as well as the old satraps, who could therefore administer their regions more efficiently. As long as the reappointed satrap stayed loyal and collected the required taxes, this arrangement worked well. However, Alexander did leave a Macedonian or a Greek in command of the armed forces in each satrapy he conquered, to make sure that security was not a problem.

After allowing his men some well-earned relaxation at Babylon, Alexander continued his progress toward Persia itself. He was joined by more reinforcements from Macedon, and took the opportunity to reorganize his army. Persia and the lands to the east were mountainous and better suited to guerrilla tactics than full-scale battles. Alexander organized his troops into smaller, more mobile units, and changed their training program accordingly.

When Alexander arrived at Susa in mid-December 331 BCE, the local satrap surrendered the city and its treasury—some 1,500 tons of silver—without a fight. Next Alexander moved on toward the Persian winter capital, Persepolis (near modern Shiraz). On the way he met resistance from a semicivilized hill tribe and the local satrap, who both tried to halt Alexan-

This is the ancient city of Persepolis in Iran. Under the control of the descendants of Achaemenes, Persepolis served as a winter capital.

der's progress through the mountain passes. In each case Alexander showed the effectiveness of his army reorganization by taking his troops through the mountains quickly and surprising his opponents. Persepolis fell to Alexander, and with it another 3,500 tons of silver. Alexander stayed at Persepolis for about four months, consolidating his gains and arranging for the careful use of his newfound financial resources.

PERSEPOLIS

"Persepolis," meaning "Persian City," is Greek for Parsa. Darius I, also known as Darius the Great, began building the palace there in 518 BCE, intending to use it as the capital of the Persian Empire. He would eventually realize that the mountainous region made it incredibly difficult to reach during the winter. Therefore, Susa, Babylon, and Ectabana were also set up as capitals.

Persepolis was mostly built using limestone. It was a city that incorporated an advanced sewage system, as well as a large cistern for catching rainwater so that it wasn't always necessary to seek water elsewhere.

Near the beginning of May 330 BCE, the vast complex of buildings that comprised the royal palace at Persepolis was burned down. According to Alexander's official story, this was the final act of revenge for the Persians' destruction of Athens 150 years before. It marked the change from the royal dynasty of Darius III, whose palace it was, to that of Alexander. However, Alexander was by now following a policy of conciliation with his new subjects in Persia and the rest of Asia. He wished to be accepted as the next rightful king of the Persian Empire rather than the king of a foreign land who had conquered them. To destroy the palace hardly suggested that he was the proper successor to Darius. The story told by other writers was that at a drunken party Alexander was persuaded by an Athenian courtesan to burn down the palace because it would be popular back in Greece. But modern archaeological evidence suggests that the rooms had been cleared of valuable possessions before the fire, which counts strongly against any sudden and arbitrary decision to destroy the palace. Uncertainty of the truth lingers.

THE LAST STAND OF DARIUS III

Darius had assembled a small army at Ecbatana (modern Hamadan), the Persian summer capital and was awaiting reinforcements from the north-east. On learning that, Alexander set off to catch

This painting depicts the fabled event of a courtesan suggesting to Alexander the Great that he burn down the royal palace at Persepolis.

him. It was essential for Alexander to take Darius out of the picture to make his own position absolutely secure. He hoped to take Darius alive and have him acknowledge the Macedonian king as the rightful ruler of Asia.

Darius hesitated, and then retreated from Ecbatana. Alexander paused at Ecbatana to establish Parmenio as commander of this strategic city. Ecbatana was in many ways the nerve center of the empire, and the key to supplying Alexander's campaigns further east.

Alexander pressed on after Darius. He took his troops, both cavalry and infantry, nearly 200 miles in eleven days in the hope of beating Darius through a mountain pass. Discovering that Darius had gone through already, Alexander waited five days to rest his men and horses. Moving through the pass, he advanced some sixty miles in two days along the edge of the desert now called the Dasht-e Kavir. When he paused for the day to forage for food he learned that Darius had been arrested by his own generals, so he set off on a final desperate chase. Traveling for two days and nights across the desert, he reached the camp where the forces with Darius had stopped the day before. Alexander learned from the locals that there was a quicker route to intercept the Persians, but it lay across a waterless part of the desert. Alexander took the toughest 500 of his men, mounted them on the remaining horses, and set off through the night. He had covered nearly forty-five miles when at dawn he saw the Persians ahead of him. Only sixty men had kept up with him, but Alexander attacked straight away. The Persians recognized the dreaded Alexander, stabbed Darius, and fled. When Alexander reached the wagon in which Darius lay, the Persian ruler was already dead.

Alexander had taken his men 250 miles in under a week, an extraordinary achievement for those times. Half the horses had died from the strain, and the rest were completely spent. But it had been in vain. Alexander took the body of Darius back to Persepolis and had him buried alongside his ancestors, as befitted a king of Persia. It was July 330 BCE, and little more than four years after invading it Alexander was the indisputable ruler of the Persian Empire. He was only twenty-six years old.

BESSUS RESISTS

Bessus, one of the Persian generals who had arrested Darius, though not one of his killers, declared himself the new king of the Persian Empire and fled to the northeast (into modern Afghanistan) to raise an army. Alexander set off to subdue this region. Bessus lacked the resources to be a major threat, but Alexander would not

When Alexander the Great finally caught up to his rival King Darius III, it was already too late.

allow him to threaten the stability of Alexander's newly won territories.

In such mountainous areas it was impossible to decide matters in a single major battle. Instead, Alexander conducted a series of smaller campaigns that took three years. He moved his forces with great speed and split them up to fight on several fronts at once, entrusting parts of his army to experienced and loyal generals like Ptolemy and Coenus. Gradually, after many sieges of mountain fortresses and some setbacks, including more injuries to himself, Alexander gained mastery of the region. Bessus was betrayed to him and executed. Alexander made treaties with the various local rulers, who were allowed to keep their positions in return for paying tribute to him. Alexander also married Roxane, the daughter of one of these leaders, who was reckoned the most beautiful woman in Asia.

PHILOTAS AND PARMENIO'S END

It was at the time of these campaigns that Alexander was made aware of a plot against his life. A Macedonian called Dimnus was trying to find men to help him kill Alexander, and when a certain Cebalinus found out about it, he reported the matter to Philotas, the son of Parmenio and commander of the Macedonian cavalry. Philotas either did nothing with the information because he thought it was false, or he had never been made aware of the situation, and so Cebalinus got the information to Alexander through someone else. Alexander was furious when he found out, and he accused Philotas of being part of the plot. When Alexander's guards attempted to arrest Dimnus, he was killed or killed himself, so there was no way of finding out who was really involved. Since Philotas was unpopular with many of Alexander's hetairoi because of his flamboyant behavior, they took this opportunity to turn against Alexander's boyhood friend. Alexander was persuaded of Philotas's guilt and had him executed.

Alexander knew that this would outrage Parmenio, whose other two sons had already been killed in Alexander's battles. Alexander may also have believed that Philotas would not have acted without his father's knowledge. With Parmenio in control of his financial reserves and a large army, Alexander could take no chances. A messenger

The marriage to Roxane was one of the events that marked the successful end of Alexander's efforts to seize control of the Persian Empire.

was dispatched with great haste and Parmenio was executed. With previous rumors of plots, Alexander had been much more trusting and tolerant. We cannot know why he had changed so much, but perhaps it was the corrupting effect of power. Alexander now split command of the Macedonian cavalry between his closest friend, Hephaestion, and Cleitus, who had saved his life at the Granicus River.

TENSION AROUND CULTURAL ACCEPTANCE

By now Alexander was the ruler of a vast empire whose people were of many different ethnic groups. His generals were almost all Macedonians, with a few Greeks. The satraps, however, were mostly Persians or other Asians. Alexander was also using troops from many parts of the empire. Many of his Macedonian troops were living with local women, even those who had wives back in Macedon. Alexander had founded numerous cities, bringing Hellenistic culture to every corner of the empire. For his people to live together in peace, it was necessary to combine all these different ethnic and cultural strands. Alexander started adding items of Persian clothing to his outfits, and he began eating Persian food. He had the sons of leading Asians educated in the Greek language and philosophy and trained them to use Macedonian weapons.

Many of the leading Macedonians did not like this policy of cultural fusion. They saw the Persians as inferior to themselves, and they could not understand why Alexander treated them with respect. They were also alienated by the way that Alexander increasingly referred to himself as the son of Amun instead of Philip. At one drunken banquet the tension flared into tragedy. An argument started between Alexander and Cleitus over the treatment of the Macedonians in the army.

An anxious Alexander fatally attacks Cleitus with a spear after an argument. Banquets weren't always safe for those who attended them.

They exchanged insults and nearly came to blows. As Ptolemy dragged Cleitus out of the room, Alexander called for his guards. When the guards, knowing this to be a harmless brawl, did not act, Alexander began to fear treason. And then, Cleitus returned to the banquet. Alexander seized a spear from a guard and ran Cleitus through, killing him. When Alexander saw that Cleitus was unarmed and had not come back to kill him, he was filled with remorse and refused to eat or drink for three days. The incident seems to have had little effect on the loyalty of his followers, for such brawling was probably not uncommon and Cleitus had been unwise for coming back. Nevertheless, we can see that Alexander feared betrayal constantly.

CHAPTER 6

ALEXANDER'S FINAL ILLNESS

Alexander the Great died how he lived: far away from home in the midst of plotting and executing war. While he may have been inexhaustible and undefeated on the battlefield, the many illnesses and injuries that he suffered would not be as impotent as his enemies. As Alexander turned his sights toward India, these would become problematic.

WAR WITH PORUS

At the start of 326 BCE, having secured the northeastern part of his empire, Alexander arrived in the northern part of modern-day Pakistan intending to extend his territories further than the Persians had done, beyond the Indus River. He knew that the local Indian rulers were too occupied with fighting each other to offer much resistance, and he planned to play them off against each other. Alexander reached the Indus in May, crossed over into the kingdom of Taxiles, who surrendered to him, and then marched on toward the kingdom of Porus, who had failed to send ambassadors to welcome him.

Porus met Alexander at the Hydaspes River (now called the Jhelum) with a large army that included two hundred war elephants. The river was too wide to ford, so Alexander would have to cross on rafts. However, the horses bolted when they smelled the elephants, making it impossible to keep them safely on the rafts. After mounting a number of attacks that were only feints meant to occupy the enemy, Alexander crossed unopposed

Alexander the Great defeats Porus and captures him at the Hydaspes River after overcoming the opposing Indian forces.

about seventeen miles upstream and then marched south to meet Porus. Making superb use of his cavalry, Alexander totally outfought the Indians. When the Macedonian infantry advanced to deal with the elephants, their discipline paid off. They were able to pick off the mahouts, leaving the elephants to their own devices. The riderless elephants panicked and did more damage to the Indian troops than to the Macedonians.

Probably two-thirds of Porus's army was slaughtered in the rout that followed, and Porus himself was captured. When Alexander asked Porus how he wished to be treated, he replied, "Like a king." So Alexander gave Porus his kingdom back to rule on Alexander's behalf. With no army left, there was little danger of Porus revolting. Alexander's victory had been absolute, although shortly after the battle his beloved warhorse Bucephalus died of exhaustion and old age.

ALEXANDER'S ARMY REFUSES INDIA

Alexander marched on toward the southwest intending to conquer the rest of India, which he had believed to be quite a small country. But it was becoming apparent that India was a vast land, and that there would be many armies to defeat. When Alexander reached the Hyphasis River (now the Beas), near modern Amritsar, he met an opponent he could not defeat—his own army.

Perhaps afraid of what they might meet in India, not knowing how far Alexander planned to advance, and weary from years of marching and fighting, the Macedonians had had enough. In a staff meeting, Coenus spoke out for the officers and men alike, giving their reasons for turning back. When this speech met with applause, Alexander must have known that he could not win. After three days shut up in his tent Alexander made sacrifices to discover the omens and, declaring that the gods were unfavorable, gave the order to turn back. It was the summer of 326 BCE. When Coenus died soon afterward, Alexander, who clearly did not hold a grudge against him for speaking up, gave him a splendid funeral.

DANGEROUS WATERS

Returning to the Indus River, Alexander sailed downstream and subdued all opposition on the

Alexander is shot through the lung with an arrow after jumping to attack the inhabitants of a walled citadel.

way. It took nine months for him to conquer the Indus valley and reach the sea, founding cities and building dockyards to promote trade along the way.

In an attack on one town, Alexander was the first to scale the wall of the citadel, and he impetuously jumped down inside. Initially only three of his bodyguards managed to join him. He killed some of the defenders before being shot through the lung with an arrow. One of his guards covered his body with the sacred shield that Alexander had been given at Troy, until finally the rest of his men forced their way into the citadel and, believing Alexander to be fatally wounded, massacred the inhabitants.

When news reached the main camp that Alexander had apparently been killed, it was

met with grief and despair. Even when a letter from Alexander was read out to say that he was alive the men did not believe it, thinking that the generals had composed it to keep up morale. As a river barge approached the camp the soldiers saw Alexander's body lying on it, and their grief was deepened until he raised a hand to wave at them. A deafening cheer went up. On reaching the riverbank, Alexander insisted on mounting his horse and riding to his tent. As he dismounted, his men rushed to touch their king and brought garlands of flowers as a sign of their joy. They had revolted at the Hyphasis River, but their adoration of Alexander was undiminished.

When he reached the mouth of the Indus on the Arabian Sea in October 325 BCE, Alexander arranged for his army's return to Persia. He sent Nearchus with the fleet to sail west along the coast and up through the Persian Gulf. This was to be a voyage of exploration of this previously uncharted coastline. Alexander himself chose to go by land with a small army across the desert of Gedrosia (modern Makran). He knew that he had to keep in contact with the fleet and help to supply it. So instead of the easier inland route he kept close to

the coast, marching mostly at night. Conditions were terrible, with no water for long stretches, and supplies ran dangerously low. Thousands died from the heat, and from exhaustion. The soldiers killed and ate whatever baggage animals did not die from the heat, which at times was over 125° F. At one point some scouts found a tiny amount of water and brought it to Alexander in a helmet. He poured it out onto the sand. All would drink or none, he declared.

The battered force finally made it to safety and joined up with the fleet and the rest of the army, which had taken the inland route.

MANAGING THE EMPIRE

Alexander punished the local satraps who had failed to send him enough supplies while in Gedrosia. During 324 BCE, Alexander progressed through the southern part of modern Iran, ending local resistance and making his way back to Susa and then on to Ecbatana. He replaced a number of satraps and generals who had abused their positions during the nearly five years since he had last been in Persia.

At Susa, Alexander arranged the marriage of many of his hetairoi to Persian brides, and he legitimized the Asian wives and children of his Macedonian troops, giving them all wedding presents. He also paid what he owed to his troops. Then he arranged for any Macedonians who were too old or unfit for military service to return to Macedon with an honorable discharge. He planned to replace them with Persians trained in the Macedonian style. This caused some discontent among the Macedonians, who felt they were being edged out. Nevertheless, Alexander continued his policy of cultural fusion throughout the army and the empire.

While at Ecbatana, Alexander's dearest friend Hephaestion died after a short illness, perhaps caused by a bout of heavy drinking. Alexander was grief-stricken. He ordered a funeral on a massive scale and laid plans for the building of a great step pyramid in Hephaestion's honor.

THE DEATH OF THE KING

Early in 323 BCE, Alexander traveled to Babylon to oversee the building of Hephaestion's pyramid and to lay plans for the invasion of Arabia.

DISEASE IN ANCIENT TIMES

This is Imhotep, an ancient Egyptian who developed a new way of practicing medicine around 5,000 years ago.

Imhotep and Hippocrates were of a similar philosophy when it came to theorizing why illness happened. They both believed that it was nature, specifically environmental factors, diet, and lifestyles, that caused disease, as opposed to supernatural forces. But these two would never meet, as Imhotep lived in ancient Egypt around 3000 BCE (and would be deified as the god of medicine), and Hippocrates lived in Greece during the 5th and 4th century BCE (and would have his contributions codified into Western medicine). Because of these theories, different ancient societies began to recognize medicine as a field separate from magic, and Alexander and his friend Hephaestion managed to survive the illnesses that they did survive because of a regimen that consisted of observation, diagnosis, and treatment.

Alexander ordered a great fleet to be constructed, planning to establish economic as well as political control of Arabia, a region with valuable resources and trade routes. During the preparations, Alexander held a banquet in honor of Nearchus, who was to command the fleet. A sequence of parties followed in the last few days of May, and Alexander began to suffer from a fever.

On May 31, Alexander had to be carried on a stretcher to make the sacrifices that he made every day, as was the duty of the king. Although his condition improved a little and he continued to give instructions for the Arabian expedition, by June 7 he had deteriorated again and was no longer able to make sacrifices. Fearing that he was already dead, his troops pushed their way into the room where

This painting shows soldiers who fought with Alexander the Great paying tribute to their dying, beloved leader.

he lay. Unable to speak and barely able to raise his head, Alexander greeted his men with his eyes as they filed past. The men insisted on saying farewell to their beloved king and general, who had shared personally in both their hardships and triumphs. Toward the evening of June 10, 323 BCE, Alexander III of Macedon, King of Asia, died at the age of thirty-two.

Some have suggested that Alexander drank himself to death. Although he was capable of heavy drinking, something the Macedonians were renowned for, there are no grounds for suggesting he was a drunkard. Others believed that one or more of his generals poisoned him, perhaps upset by the policy of cultural fusion, but there is no evidence of that. Another theory is that Alexander died of a disease, either malaria or typhoid. But malaria is transmitted through mosquitoes that weren't found where he died. And the latter would only have been possible in a widespread outbreak, due to the infectious way in which typhoid is transmitted. In 2014, another theory was put forth by Dr. Leo Schep from the National Poisons Centre in New Zealand. Alexander may have drunk a poisonous wine fermented from the innocuous-looking

Veratrum album plant, an herbal treatment that the Greeks often used. Death in this way may have been accidental, or an orchestrated assassination.

THE EMPIRE DISSOLVES

In Babylon, the Macedonian army elected Alexander's half-brother Philip Arrhidaeus as the new king. What followed was a struggle for power between Alexander's generals, who split the empire between themselves. Olympias murdered Philip Arrhidaeus and declared Alexander's son, born to Alexander's wife Roxane after his death, King Alexander IV. But Olympias had made too many enemies, and she and Alexander IV were soon murdered themselves. Antipater died in 319 BCE after a short period in which he dominated the empire.

In a complicated series of civil wars, a threefold division of power eventually emerged. Antigonus ruled the Macedon kingdom. Macedon eventually became a province of the Roman Empire in 146 BCE. Most of Alexander's empire eventually came under the control of Seleucus, a lesser commander. The Seleucid dynasty lasted for about 150 years before these territories broke up under

pressure from Rome and the nomadic tribes from central Asia. The longest lasting successor of Alexander was Ptolemy, who took control of Egypt. His last descendant was Cleopatra, from whom the Romans took Egypt in 30 BCE.

Alexander the Great was a complicated figure who alternated between destructive tendencies and an unchangeable appreciation of those he wanted to dominate. In a dozen years his temperament and drive would alter the face of the world. He created a custom in many countries that soldiers have regular training before going into battle; spread Hellenistic culture and the culture of the peoples he conquered from Afghanistan and back; and showed the world that India was a bigger land with more kingdoms than was known.

absolute monarch An individual who rules a state with no obligation to consider the advice or needs of others in decision making.

Achilles A hero from Greek mythology who was the mightiest warrior in the Trojan War.

Amun The king of the gods in Egyptian mythology. The Greeks usually regarded him as being the same as their god Zeus.

causeway A raised way across wet ground or water.

cavalry Soldiers who fought on horseback.

Dionysus The Greek god of wine, the theater, and ecstatic experience, who is also the son of Zeus.

flank The side or wing of a group of people.

garrison A body of troops stationed to defend a stronghold, usually in a town or fort.

Heracles The greatest of the heroes in Greek mythology because of his strength and bravery, and also the son of Zeus.

hetairoi The name given to the wealthy and powerful landowners who acted as the king of Macedon's senate, who would normally make up the generals and other army officers.

infantry Foot soldiers.

mahout Elephant drivers of Porus's army.

oracle Usually a priest or priestess in Greek mythology through which humans were able to seek the advice of a god.

Persia Now in modern Iran, the part of the Persian Empire that the king and most of his satraps came from.

phalanx An infantry formation relying on the closeness of fighters to collectively use their shields for effective protection while they advance with their weapons.

primary source A source that serves as a direct witness or that offers direct proof of something. For example, the transcript of a speech as a means of proving what a person said is a primary source.

satrap The governor of a province in the Persian Empire who had full authority in both civil and military matters and was responsible for supplying troops and taxes to the king.

satrapy A province of the Persian Empire.

secondary source A source that examines direct evidence of or a direct witness to an event. For example, a news article about a crime that contains an interview of a witness is a secondary source.

siege To surround a place to cut off the delivery of supplies as a means of forcing surrender.

siege engine A device that is meant to attack, break through, or bypass a fortification during a siege.

Zeus The king of the gods in Greek mythology who had many responsibilities in addition to controlling weather (especially thunder).

American Classical League
Miami University
Oxford, OH 45056
Phone: (513) 529-7741
Website: http://www.aclclassics.org
This organization supports the study of classical languages in the United States and Canada.

Canadian Museum of History
100 Laurier Street
Gatineau, Québec K1A 0M8
Canada
Phone: (800) 555-5621
Website: http://www.historymuseum.ca
This museum offers historical exhibits that reveal the ancient and recent past to contemporary audiences.

Institute for the Study of the Ancient World (ISAW)
15 East 84th Street
New York, NY 10028
Phone: (212) 992-7800
Website: http://isaw.nyu.edu
ISAW's mission is to enable the study of economic, religious, political, and cultural connections between ancient civilizations by examining texts, artifacts, and environmental observations.

International Plutarch Society
Department of History
Utah State University
0710 Old Main Hill
Logan, UT 84322-0710
Website: http://ips.ploutarchos.org
This society is dedicated to furthering the study of Plutarch and his writings. It keeps track of and shares information about conferences, publications, and news of interest.

Museum of Classical Antiquities
Desmarais Building
55 Laurier Ave. East, 3th Floor
Ottawa, ON Canada
Phone: (613) 562-5800
Website: http://arts.uottawa.ca/cla-srs/en/museum
This museum displays artifacts that help visitors of all ages gain a greater understanding of what types of difficulties governments, private citizens, and visitors frequently faced.

Onassis Cultural Center New York
Olympic Tower
645 Fifth Avenue
New York, NY 10022

Website: http://www.onassisusa.org
Exhibitions, events, and online engagement from the Onassis Cultural Center offer a lens through which visitors can explore Greek culture.

WEBSITES

Because of the changing nature of internet links, Rosen Publishing has developed an online list of websites related to the subject of this book. This site is updated regularly. Please use this link to access this list:

http://www.rosenlinks.com/LANW/alexander

Anson, Edward M. *Alexander the Great: Themes and Issues*. London, UK: Bloomsbury, 2013.

Hosein, Ann. *The History of Technology*. New York, NY: Brittanica Educational Publishing, 2016.

Fox, Robin Lane. *Alexander the Great*. New York, NY: Penguin Group, 2013.

Howe, Timothy, Erin Garvin, and Graham Wrightson, eds. *Greece, Macedon and Persia*. Oxford, UK: Oxbow Books, 2015.

Kuiper, Kathleen, ed. *Ancient Greece: From the Archaic Period to the Death of Alexander the Great*. New York, NY: Britannica Educational Publishing, 2010.

Martell, Hazel Mary, and Cleo Kuhtz. *Ancient Greek Civilization*. New York, NY: Rosen Publishing, 2009.

Nossov, Konstantin. *Ancient and Medieval Siege Weapons: A Fully Illustrated Guide to Siege Weapons and Tactics*. Lanham, MD: Lyons Press, 2012.

Spivey, Nigel. *The Classical World: The Foundations of the West and the Enduring Legacy of Antiquity*. New York, NY: Pegasus Books, 2016.

Thornton, Stephanie. *The Conqueror's Wife: A Novel of Alexander the Great*. New York, NY: Penguin Group, 2015.

Worthington, Ian. *By the Spear: Philip II, Alexander the Great, and the Rise and Fall of the Macedonian Empire*. Oxford, UK: Oxford University Press, 2014.

Young, Andrew. *The Lost Book of Alexander the Great*. Yardley, PA: Westholme Publishing, 2014.

Anson, Edward M. *Alexander's Heirs: The Age of the Successors*. New York, NY: Wiley-Blackwell, 2014.

Arrian, Plutarch, Quintus Curtius Rufus, Tania Gergel, and Michael Wood. *Alexander the Great: The Brief Life and Towering Exploits of History's Greatest Conqueror—As Told by His Original Biographers*. New York, NY: Penguin Group, 2004.

Cartledge, Paul. *Ancient Greece: A Very Short Introduction*. Oxford, UK: Oxford University Press, 2011.

Fox, Robin J. Lane *Brill's Companion to Ancient Macedon*. Leiden, The Netherlands: Brill, 2015.

Garland, Robert. *Wandering Greeks: The Ancient Greek Diaspora from the Age of Homer to the Death of Alexander the Great*. Princeton, NJ: Princeton University Press, 2014.

Hamilton, J. R. *Alexander the Great*. London, UK: Hutchinson University Library, 1973.

Hammond, Nicholas. *Alexander the Great: King, Commander and Statesman*. Bristol, UK: The Bristol Press, 1989.

Historyofmacedonia.org. "Philip of Macedon." Retrieved August 26, 2016, http://www.historyofmacedonia.org/AncientMacedonia/PhilipofMacedon_last.html.

Holloway, April. "Who or what killed Alexander the Great?" Ancient Origins. January 12, 2014, www.ancient-origins.net/news-history-archaeology/have-scientists-solved-2000-year-old-mystery-death-alexander-great-001213.

Lendering, Jona. "Phalanx and Hoplites." Livius.org. Retrieved August 26, 2016, http://www.livius.org/pha-phd/phalanx/phalanx.html.

Mark, Joshua J. "The Greek Phalanx." *Ancient History EncyclopediaTM*. January 18, 2012, http://www.ancient.eu/article/110.

Mark, Joshua J. "Persepolis." *Ancient History EncyclopediaTM*. September 2, 2009, http://www.ancient.eu/persepolis.

Pothos.org. "Darius III (Codomannus)." Retrieved August 23, 2016, http://www.pothos.org/content/index.php?page=darius-iii.

Roisman, Joseph, ed. *Alexander the Great: Ancient and Modern Perspectives*. Lexington, MA: D.C. Heath and Co., 1995.

Serageldin, Ismail. "Ancient Alexandria and the Dawn of Medical Science." *Global Cardiology Science & Practice*. 2013.4 (2013): 395–404. PMC. http://www.ncbi.nlm.nih.gov/pmc/articles/PMC3991212/.

7wonders. "The Lighthouse of Alexandria, Egypt." Retrieved August 24, 2016, http://www

.7wonders.org/africa/egypt/alexandria/lighthouse-of-alexandria.

Woods, Michael and Mary B. *Seven Wonders of the Ancient World*. Minneapolis, MN: Twenty-First Century Books, 2008.

Worthington, Ian. *Alexander the Great: A Reader.* London, UK: Routledge, 2012.

A

B

C

L

M

N

O

P

ABOUT THE AUTHORS

Beatriz Santillian earned her B.A. in English in 2003, and her Ph.D in history in 2009. She is a fan of all things to do with ancient history and loves to learn about artifacts from the past. Santillian writes on topics to do with culture, technology, and change, and she also writes software in her spare time. She lives in Rochester, New York, with her daughter.

Bernard Randall read ancient history and philosophy at St. Andrew's University, Scotland, before moving to the University of Edinburgh, Scotland, for a master's degree in classics. He completed his doctorate on Greece, focusing on the fifth century BCE, at the University of Manchester, England. He has taught Greek and Roman history at the University of Manchester, and Greek history for the Open University. His main research interest is the history of Sparta up to 400 BCE. His other interests include early church history and theology, rugby, the Discworld novels of Terry Pratchett, and juggling.

PHOTO CREDITS

Cover, p. 3 Curioso/Shutterstock.com; cover (background), pp. 6–7 Mansell/The LIFE Picture Collection/Getty Images; p. 11 DEA/A. DE GREGORIO/De Agostini Picture Library/Getty Images; p. 15 Universal History Archive/Universal Images Group/Getty Images; p. 16 Dorling Kindersley/Getty Images; p. 19 Heritage Images/Hulton Archive/Getty Images; pp. 26–27 Salle Alane Reason/Exactostock-4268/Superstock; p. 28 Print Collector/Hulton Archive/Getty Images; p. 32 Atlaspix/Alamy Stock Photo; p. 35 The Art Institute of Chicago, IL, USA/The Leonora Hall Gurley Memorial Collection/Bridgeman Images; p. 38 DEA PICTURE LIBRARY/De Agostini/Getty Images; p. 41 PHAS/Universal Images Group/Getty Images; pp. 42, 60 DEA/A. DAGLI ORTI/De Agostini Picture Library/Getty Images; p. 47 Three Lions/Hulton Archive/Getty Images; pp. 51, 70, 92–93 © North Wind Picture Archives; pp. 52–53, 63 Hulton Archive/Getty Images; pp. 56–57 Heckepics/iStock/Thinkstock; p. 67 Anton Ivanov/Shutterstock.com; pp. 73, 79 Ivy Close Images/Alamy Stock Photo; pp. 76–77 Musee des Beaux-Arts, Rouen, France/Bridgeman Images; pp. 82–83 MCLA Collection/Alamy Stock Photo; pp. 86–87 © iStockphoto.com/ZU 09; p. 91 Science and Society/SuperStock; interior pages background images © iStockphoto.com/kikkalek5050 (sky), Triff/Shutterstock.com (map).

Designer: Brian Garvey; Editor: Bernadette Davis; Photo Researcher: Karen Huang